The Heart Never Pretends to Be a Beautiful Muscle

poems by

Amanda Hartzell

Finishing Line Press
Georgetown, Kentucky

The Heart Never Pretends to Be a Beautiful Muscle

For Carson. For Tegan.

Copyright © 2023 by Amanda Hartzell
ISBN 979-8-88838-210-3 First Edition
All rights reserved under International and Pan-American Copyright Conventions. No part of this book may be reproduced in any manner whatsoever without written permission from the publisher, except in the case of brief quotations embodied in critical articles and reviews.

ACKNOWLEDGMENTS

Poems originally appear in the following publications:

"Maybe Antelope," "Ocean City," "This Body Is Not"—*Cathexis Northwest Press*, 2020.
"Villains," "The Industry," "Date Night"—*The Knicknackery*, 2020.
"Unknowing"—*Petrichor Journal*, 2020 (Best of the Net nominee).
 "El Paso in Space"—*High Shelf Press*, 2021.
"Real Work"—*Kestrel*, 2021.
"The Witch and Dead President Visit Rockport"—*Kestrel*, 2021.
"Monster with a Name"—*Midway Journal*, 2021.
"Everything I Learned About Women in Movies"—*West Trade Review*, 2021.
"X's"—*Wild Roof Journal*, 2021.
"Campfire Story"—*Qu Literary Magazine*, 2021.
"Delicates"—*The Worcester Review*, 2021.
"Strawberry in pandemics"—*Variant Literature Journal*, 2021.
"Vinegar"—*Ember Chasm Review*, 2021 (2021 Poetry Winner).

Thank you to my parents and sisters for valuing each creative pursuit. To my husband, Jeb, for holding down the fort wherever we build it—I love you. To my son and daughter who infuse this life with more light and glee than I ever thought possible. And to the talented writers and creators I am lucky enough to call friends, thank you for your reading, edits, and support: Thea Engst, Rachael Inciarte, Kristian Macaron, Jon McConnell, T.J. Staneart, Sonja Vitow, and especially Margaret Wakelee.

Publisher: Leah Huete de Maines
Editor: Christen Kincaid
Cover Art: Vanessa Barragao
Author Photo: Amanda Hartzell
Cover Design: Elizabeth Maines McCleavy

Order online: www.finishinglinepress.com
also available on amazon.com

Author inquiries and mail orders:
Finishing Line Press
PO Box 1626
Georgetown, Kentucky 40324
USA

Table of Contents

PART I

Villains 2
Maybe Antelope 3
This Body Is Not 4
The Industry 5
Date Night 6
A Present 8
El Paso in Space 9
I Never Want to Leave 11
The Witch and Dead President Visit Rockport 12
Rip Current 13
Sleight Orca 14
Melatonin 15
Campfire Story 16
Delicates 17
Vinegar 18
Girls Explain 19
Growing Season 20
Monster with a Name 21

PART II

Unknowing 23
Hometowns 24
Real Work 25
Twelve Weeks 26
First Lights 27
Namesake 28
X's 29
RSVP 30
Leftovers 31
In a Dream About My Son 32
Last Orchard 33
Too Rough 34
Strawberry in Pandemics 35
Everything I Learned About Women in Movies 36

I.

*Be careful, says the body from its shape
like a body, if this is the story you want to tell.*

Villains

Rooting for bad weather is like

crushing on the villains in movies
and if this dooms me drag me to hell

then take my pants off. The prettier you

are, the uglier I am, the more powerful
us both on a dark and stormy night. Are

there ambulances, stand-offs, a child

leaping from a burning building?
Gangsters eating ice cream, a sad loner

with a gun and bad grades — or you, a cigar,

magic words in a New England forest
ablaze in the snow. I'm here too.

Someone in a mirror is watching

only themselves. Someone is starving
to death for the sake of feeling better.

If I feel you I'm in a fairy tale where no one is safe.

People only transform into monsters when
the wolf eats open eyes, the zombie licks

tongue. We kept both as pets. Once I saw a hand crawl

across the bed but it was just a pillow, it was just
what I didn't say in the dark.

Maybe Antelope

This place is full of antelope who will eat
popsicles with you. They are better

than cats and way better than your
first boyfriend. They are better kissers

even but cold because of the popsicles.
It was the Fourth of July seven years ago

burnt fields waking up remembering.
Firecrackers shiver in grass glowing

in plastic. If you light them they scream.
If you don't light them they scream also.

No one is waiting for you to do anything.
Have you met the antelope yet? Not all of them

are antelope. In case of prairie grass fire
please stand on all fours and keep blinking

the shapes back into your eyes. Make a sound like
a person. Try your best to be still and maybe even real.

This Body Is Not

This body I came with is really doing
a spectacular job. Cleaned itself
this morning, sat poking the soft flesh.
Made orange juice, made a joke, took itself
into the garden to remark how bright and green
things were, not exploding even though
we could only hear the explosions. The body
wondered if instead it could feel good and
conducted experiments, many involving hair,
before determining yes it could. It ranks pleasure

on a scale of expected-to-blistering,
and that's nice I think, that the worst pleasure
can be is expected. Bullets and a throat arrive
in the garden, new friends. We show them out
and give directions. They stumble arm-in-arm.
The body has now decided to engage
in salutes, escapades, missteps, regrets,
feats, apologies, strategies. If you squint it looks
like dancing, ice cream, moonlight.
If you don't, it looks a terror.

You'd think this would take some time
but it doesn't. Hardly anything does.
To think a thing is the most exhausting part.

While the body is briefly occupied what's left of me
goes out and traps a yellow bird with a box.
The sound it makes shut up inside lets me know it's real.
The shaking lets me know there's a sound, and
that the sound is packaged in the shape of a bird.
The body is not interested in gifts, so it says, but this
is not a gift, no promise or comfort.
Just listen. Just watch.
I open the box slowly while the body
watches. Inside is a shape of a bird

but it is not a bird. It is the explosions.
Think carefully, says the body from its shape
like a body, if this is the story you want to tell.

The Industry

We took home our leftovers and they gave us the waitress too.
She wouldn't fit in our stomachs or in one of the styrofoam boxes.
She attends to the boxes. We are drunk trying to sleep,
hearing her open and reopen the fridge with gentle pucker smacks:

Hello how are you tonight?
How did it taste?
Can I get you anything else?

Light cools her face. Her fingers on a lipped
edge shine with grease that made
the dead animal delicious.

I go downstairs and bring her up.
I put her down in the bed between us.
She smells hopeful like a pet.
I call her by her nametag but she does not respond.

The dead animal in my stomach turns to her. Fond recognition.
She tucks in her tips on the pillow. Crinkled old men.
Please write a review she says as her arms fall off to hold me.

How is it tonight?
How did you taste?
Can you give me anything else?

Date Night

Tonight, leave your box.

Have dinner in a magic eye
and stare it into sense. My hand
on the napkin, red glop. Your eyes
on the waiter, blue curtains. Everyone in love

with the squiggle, our never baby. Our knives

say delicious things. Outside the window lives
citronella and gasoline. Moths offer decaf and mints.
After the pad thai and laminated menus, go home
a long way.

You're so wet.

Dry off. Be startled.
Hold the stolen silverware near your chest
and hear it chitter. Why are knives so beautiful
when they leave the table? Maybe it's theft

or seeing hardness at night.

If your stomach hurts it was definitely
the food, not what you said. Pass bars and neon
smokers, jackets on fire and skirts like that one state
you'd never visit, turnpike horrible. Stop. Someone has a tattoo

they'd love to tell you about. Cartoons keep us light

and immaculate in the dark. Draw me and I'll draw you. I left
my outline at the restaurant and will call them about it tomorrow. For now
take whiskey shots with a rabbit and its third eye, itching to get off
an arm. The sound in the bar grips the ceiling. Olives and ski ball.

Beer beer beer. Kiss in a bathroom like thieves.

Everyone on the sidewalk stays high
in little museums of friendship. Drumrolls
and outtakes. Late night details glossed over.
Did it happen: the hurricane warning, gum on your sandal?

The rabbit is back, sloppy and intimate

as a classroom diorama. We place the knives
in the shoebox and remember our mints. Don't touch.
Must touch. If we're still hungry, eat in a glass room
with a stranger. If service is terrible, eat the glass.

A Present

Arriving home a wooden box waits
in the center of the rug. It smells like a wet
vacation, unwanted swim in the lake at seven.
Maybe it is a phone booth. A time machine.
An elevator to the end of the world.

The hands that built it are steady and wise
and terrified, the box so tall the hands
cut a neat square in the ceiling and this box
knows it. The box grows hungry
wider and taller every day.

Sleeping upstairs with a hole in the floor
is strange, box needling through, more so
for the guests I bring up there. We sing
or dance or watch window planes
blinking to the airport or lay

undressed with wind blowing out
the yellow shades and we try
to be happy but we still don't know
what the box is for, except
when listening to the screams.

El Paso in Space

Do not suffocate. Do not send your children
across the border on tricycles intended

for outer space. A name can make you
less a person, more a crater.

Bunker down in the orbiter eyes north
with everything designed to burn beneath you.

Greetings from interplanetary dust, from
its spectral frost on asylum and prickly pears.

Where else to go but towards inevitable
uncertain dark—even the youngest sense

meteors in El Salvador, then a hopeful wreck.
The world ends in spectacular blues

and citrus, in a picture from your childhood
cutting into sprinkles on birthday cake.

The one blanket given is woven from stardust
and traded by gangs for milk. What's English

for America? Do you need your blanket?
If you're hungry and cold

list right now the birthdays of anyone
who has ever touched you.

Intimacy is a shock to what the body trusts—
Don't comprehend body. Understand space

spreads into a deeper gaze. No dates and
no end. Just unwashed elbows in elbows. Suddenly

deepest sea makes sense, the windowless
room and its bodies in silver wait,

all pressure and anonymity.
Brachiopods in desert. Boulders cut

from hickory by glaciers. Limestone
as conduit, a uterus in the warehouse.

There is nothing left but everything. A howl
forgotten in a cage. Counting by twos.

If the world ends without cake or children stand
up tall, burn the pictures, learn foreign words.

I Never Want to Leave

i.
Not everything is human.
Not everything is a healing
sea or temple sworn by new
ghosts to be. I never want to leave

this season. Who actually believes
blood and bone is how to experience
the world? This morning I found

a dead rabbit in the shed half
eaten by crows full of opals.

ii.
Who actually believes the world
is how to experience blood and bone?

I never want to leave this human.
Not every season heals the rabbit
and finds dead crows in the temple.

Morning ghosts swear by
opals and swim out as far
as salt takes them.
Who actually believes? The world.

iii.
The temple swears
you will experience ghosts.
Not all salt heals
dead rabbits and crows.

But this morning I found
a shed full of opals
one for each broken bone.

Who actually wants to leave
when the ghosts are thirsty?

If blood comes for the world, swim out.

The Witch and Dead President Visit Rockport

They arrive at a pink and brick coastal town pummeled
by the Atlantic, too cold and brittle with lady slippers to swim.

The president has been dead long enough.
No one remembers his birthday or how he takes his coffee.

The witch shops for scrimshaws, ancient and ornate like her dreams.
She wants to hang one above her futon as if it might explain

why she cannot swim or wrap presents or why
she can't warm up no matter how she burns.

The dead president does a breaststroke at high tide.
He searches for a whale with valves large enough

to crush any man composed of small
catastrophes and keepsakes.

Tide in lungs he remembers being young eating diner
over-easies and dancing with his mother and drunk aunts.

When he is gone the witch wanders alone. She believes
the dead president knows a whale is just a place.

She believes that heaven boils blue with suns. She gets
serious and kills some sweetness. She finds a barn

on the pier and inside are paintings of other barns.
She buys one with doors open to fields of snow.

Lying on her futon much later she notices in
the painting dark shapes moving behind trees.

Most likely they are animals or shapes
that believe they are animals.

Rip Current

Outside the dark is a whole mouth

of the sea. A vacation car on gravel moves
the teeth. If you're hungry enough for taffy

you can eat through one mouth into another

and your teeth go bad at some other age
an island and spoken life away.

In that one, curtains. In this one, fat starfish
waving hello. The hotel holds sand and ladies

slippers in pastel frames. All the rooms

identical except for the chlorine children,
so alike they go for pizza with different families.

At night awake with lamp posts we visit fortune tellers—

we're so bored and hopeful. We're so smooth and
devastated. There is light on your eyelids like I

have never seen. From the hotel window

a crowd creates ruckus on the shore. If you squint
you can tell it's just one person, breaking bottles.

Sand is very small glass and August tinier, especially after

we find the stingray rotting in the froth. Fly in gulls,
white and black. They descend on boardwalk fries while

immobile glorious leeches cheer on. If you know

someone who's drowned, do they ever swim
back to you with ice cream?

Sleight Orca
> *After the orca, Tahlequah ('two is enough"), who carried her calf*

In Deception Pass the orca still carries
her young corpse. A beautiful island,
this grief magician. Watch closely.
Follow each sleight of hand. Stacking cups

turn my heart into another muscle—one
I can clench. It glows in the dark. The trick
to love is love at nothing. I love you so
you exist. Yellow birds exploding

in the amphitheater. Bubbles rising
in the tank. I love you so you pretend
you're real. You know the future
is more than fire and siren, gut punch and ghost.

One trick to reassurance: respond
by name, turn back when called even just
to be sawed in half. Who doesn't covet
some hocus pocus? A way to roll back rock

from cave or peel card from orange. To live
underwater. My grief magician bears
a wet hat holding hunger. The doves are gone,
the ribbon back in my mouth. For my first trick

I will need an assistant. For my second. For my second.

Melatonin

Welcome don't resist citronella and hairspray when walking into the house of a great aunt never met, and the screened porch racket of her parakeets and clink of her four-easy-payments-of bracelet and her labored collection of soup spoons and how she says *you're the spitting image of your mother, and of my sister before she ran off with that truck driver in Cleveland, oh you look just like the woman in that sleep aid commercial,* the one who discusses her problems softly to a glowing moth and lays in bed smiling while a huge orchard grows overnight in the window, and maybe she wakes at dawn and picks crabapples but probably she just sleeps, oh just like her, those women clutching love and troubles, like everyone other than myself.

Campfire Story

You are a campfire and the bear
in the woods we were warned about.
That VHS tape with all the white lines.

You are the overplayed movie about
the campers who befriend a wild
bear by sheer magic and only one

of them gets eaten. You are the berries
in the bear's stomach the eaten camper
strings together to make a rope

to climb back out of the bear
chanting a tune his father sang
so in bad moments, like a bear's throat,

he is really in a kitchen toes on tile
watching his father love the radio.
Then suddenly you are the bear's teeth

mouth wide with surprise as the camper emerges
healthy though a little sticky and slathered
in berry juice. You are the flowing canteen

and applause, the newspaper headlines
the forest that disappears in darkness
only to return the next day and the next.

You, campfire black and cold as a shrine.

Delicates

Every day wake up and care

for the bomb in your throat.
Go to work. Set the table.

Patience. Be delicate

but know an argument implodes
a new home, birthday confetti

and celebration dinners

how one can look at another saying
here is our life, my life

so much better before you.

Aren't you only wire and charge
in an unmarked box, staring up

at an old stranger who said yes

to a call and now doesn't know
what to do with your fine disaster

cold and live.

Vinegar

I woke up and found you overnight
became a small bowl of vinegar
glistening and barely
indenting the pillow.

You expect me to carry you
to the dresser and watch me
undress, dress, tuck in sheets.
You refuse to go back into the bottle.

What can anyone do? I hide napkins
and cultivate slightest pang of hunger.
Throw out utensils and every single platter—
paper plates and fine china—that does not contain you.

But all you want is to sit at the open window
so your new body can reflect telephone poles
and apartments vacant for scrambling
children and the backyard we dug up.

Mud and concrete slabs, hopeful
objects still wrapped in tarp.
We overlooked the wreckage.
Just imagine: Fire pit.

Swing chair. Small pond
with speckled fish that know, unlike
our hands fumbling for flavor and heat,
how to sleep for months in ice.

Girls Explain

Winter violence
worn by young girls.
Does this matter?
Explain bells.
Explain girls.
Explain very old trembling.

An echo
inside a hill
still does not leave
my hand on you
a different hand or
a different body.

The bodies in the hill
are types of hills
and my hand a type
of ringing.
Close your eyes.
All the shapes go round.

To be worth anything
location needs distance.
Let's dig here
until the chimes
explain where in me
you've buried all my hands.

Tell me a secret.
You can lie.
Pretend you've lost something.
A tree is a tree in winter
is you gone to seed in winter
is you casting a dark forest in me.

Growing Season

Take manure and perennials
and reap nothing. Keep it wild

overgrown and always arriving
through hard frost, stubborn and green.

Become the whole forest teeming
with yellow eyes navigating smoke.

Abandon each brain, that canopy
on fire. We're alive or

something close. Forgo water,
face crackle and blaze

overcoming the harvest beneath
its embarrassment of stars.

Monster with a Name

Forget everything today.
What death we're on, our locked
room bodies, how outside windows
swell marches beneath raised batons.
Forget under the bed breathe monsters
who only know how to pronounce your name.

Once upon a lie we set a forest
on fire, naked and delighted.
But it grew back.
Each tree exploding from sap
boiled inside—forget it.
Wolves and crows fled. Shut windows.

Who needs air? This is not defeatist.
Just remember: birds destroy
each other's eggs and the heart
never pretends to be
a beautiful muscle.

II.

*Among soap and grime, come out
like dew and wildflower*

Unknowing

Even horses know they are just horses.
Even gulls know distinction from falling.
Even forests know how to disturb, lose
daughters, permit fields their sudden light.
Even the dog knows I'm leaving.
The door broken from both sides by dust
and lightning. Even I know the worst thing.

Light creeps in. And here: if you stare too
long at unripe fruit, pistil and petal,
photos of lovers before you swarmed
into their bodies waving matchsticks—
what's to see except the greed and fire
in your own heart, beating against wind,
that unknowing monster we call heart.

Hometowns

Jersey returns in two forms:
the shore and hooves
in the pine barrens.
Tiny liquor stores
with bars and children tucked
in the back, an unseen naval base,
stubbly yards of rocks
with dogs ignoring their names
pacing the chainlinks.
Radio yelling how they love
this team so much they hate it.
And I have only felt that way
about a person or two,
losing backdoor keys
and tipping a glass into
my mouth to say goodbye.

The carpet and stairwells
span small and frantic here
as all the people I no longer know
wait on me to come to dinner.
I'd like to fold the appetizers in napkins
and give them to my favorite dead dog
but there are so many wet noses.
In gold and black slivers of pine
comes wind so furious it builds
and crashes like undertow and salt
threatening and intimate but not mine.
I'd rather stand on the frosting porch
with mulch and crushed eggshells
watching bats deliver their dark bodies
in blind arcs between the trees
going on forever in the dusk.

Real Work

Who took the trash out and bought the wilted flowers and forgot to clean the coffee filter and now there's mold who took the dog out and at what darkening time who called back my mother who was nice to the cashier with the weird makeup who said homelessness makes the parks look bad who asked the other to have a real opinion for once who cleaned out the car and found all those baby socks who turned on the tv when the whole house shone gold with a headache who forgot to shave who said that's a firefly that's an expensive drink that's a scary thought who checked flights who sang all the wrong lyrics but could tell you about the bassist who cried at the wedding who blacked out who found that show before everyone else who tolerated this birch tree who sat at a table together silent working on private worlds

Twelve Weeks

When saying goodbye
who wants to be looking into
a muddy trench, undoing a bow
or rebuilding gentle bloody organs

that once glided onstage in limelight
knowing how to pirouette and fight nicely.
When saying goodbye bring all
the birds hoarse from hollowing out

homes in a canyon. Bring the snow
sweetened with candies melted
to a mouth. Bring softest sheets meeting
the strangest bodies, all crave and hope,

all swell and swarm. When you take
the child's fabric that belongs to you, and take
it away, hear the single easy song
that swishes between the creases.

The tea I brewed this morning
smoked on in a March window
for years and hours.

First Lights

In early hours when sun
breaks open morning like
a peeled orange
studded with glass

bodies move in rooms
all slope and shiver
with windows flushed
from coffee and other heat

then dissolve in cold new air.
Much easier to pretend this is a movie
strangers beautiful and tragic but
worth every cry and each cake.

My son tried to pick the freckle
off my face, held the dog's paw
when I said it was bedtime, cried
when a sandwich fell off the bench.

On wet days and in nightfall, flickering
credits appreciate the fade and
the way it's selfish to love and cup
hands around smallest warmth.

Namesake

What to call this love
the I lose track

of my body when your
body is in my eyes love

the I blink and here swells
a room with clementines

and a panting lapdog outside
wheat fields darkening

with August rain you hear
coming the way a son is loved

easily when still growing inside
a red castle—blueberry love

but sweeter and smaller
because you have never

touched me when I bled or made
me soup after I howled how

these city porches make me
dead and so one of us will bring

in magnolia leaves
from a vicious frost

so this winter house
once stripped down

blooms with each leaf's
impatient spider love

X's

This ends with fire but first — backseat,
brownstones and moonlit alleys.
Clothes soaked by an early snow
burying unsuspecting foothill towns.
Easy to believe people
we love are set on fire
or glow despite.

Twirl through night just to be deposited
at a door, touching your new body but still
begging the young ghosts under skin:
*Give me a chance to tear a forest apart
with my teeth.* Small animal, bright-eyed.
Soil in matted paws. Nitrogen hovers
above a warming den.

A thousand years later,
not so long, and after
the strangest
and most delicate dream
where the body belongs
to itself, wake up hungry, ember
under each shredded claw.

RSVP

In a world before I became a shape
in your bed I watched a son
skin a doe and walked as far
back into the forest as I could.
Shimmer and technique, muscle
beyond spirit, upside-down to drain.
All this for party's sake. Next time
let's show up drunk already.
Each present wrapped stays

more desired unopened so
kick off shoes and take ones
we wish we wore home.
Kiss in a stranger's bathroom
among soap and grime, come out
like dew and wildflower.

Leftovers

First gather pits of stone
fruit and rinds in empty

tumblers. Next the jar
with buttons separated

from our frayed coats. Pluck toast
crusts from yesterday's plates

and from the drawer dull razor
heads. Save bucket after bucket

of bath water, suds and dirt
a cold film on each surface.

Find still: movie stubs, dried
pens, wadded paper in slacks.

Outside in winter soil scatter
eggshells from years of morning

scrambles, white among roots
of last season's crocus.

Each scrap exhausted, hunted
down in a house without

one of us in it
this leftover world.

In a Dream About My Son

I took him to a gallery in Seattle and we roved over painted bowls of oranges, skeleton keys, thatched roofs and amateur ballerinas. Flesh and fabric wet and rioting. He didn't hold my hand. He made up his own name. He will always be derived from me but apart. Jackets under jacket and sun beneath spotlight. When I said I liked the figs, he saw a basket of stones.

Last Orchard

And other times circling back
        there remain only cavities—
                bedroom emptied of photos
fruit bowl with a single orange.
        Necessary to take an entire

                trapeze and its painted act and
        every sea under spyglass
                handfuls of wilted marigolds
        and scatter them
                like what they are:

a slew of trinkets from the story
        you tell yourself
                deposited
        either to rot or
                reassemble in dreams.

                Only then walk out.
        Bite orange straight
        through rind and when
                locking gates and throwing
up dust remember

        the smile from a stranger
                that explodes in lungs a thousand
different groves your sunlit
        body might have held.

Too Rough

I just wanted to check if I was too rough
with you. I just wanted to check if

you knew about late frosts. I just wanted
to wonder what you'll plant this year

in your strange new city. I just wanted
tomatoes and zucchini and doesn't

zinfandel sound better as a flower?
Whiskey a nightshade, gin a succulent.

I just wanted to see if you'd take
this call since we're just another

two people, imagining gardens.

Strawberry in Pandemics

Come sit in my hotel room
and scratch my head.
I want to be a pet

who has a pet
and room service
parfaits and mimosas

and flaky bread with bubbles
from kneading and waiting.
Rip green from strawberries,

their seeds on the outside
not seeds at all but ovaries
hiding a seed inside.

If that makes you want them less
cover each in chocolate so we don't
have to rehash how living doubles just

to depart from itself, how it returns ashamed,
or anything besides the moonset and whether
anyone on this speck will stop getting sick.

I'll take you for a walk and you will take
me for one. Sniff the damp air and pour
our bodies out on sidewalks.

We nod at each passerby
like they know us gently enough
to pick seeds from our teeth.

Everything I Learned About Women in Movies

Reclaim grace from the imposters: chiffon
dresses and crosses in dust, sheep dazed
in a field above a town of sentimental whores.
Forget film stars cinching waists in gray,
the gymnasts lithe explosions of chalk.
Leave the debutantes at dinner tables.
Fresh from powder rooms, shining in knife light.

Let grace run screaming to heavy ghosts.

But stop me if you've seen this movie before.
Get to the part when silhouette undoes shadow,
the scene hands wash down to whitest bone.

Skip over the drowning and beatings repeated
and convenience store fires, the headaches
turned heartaches of savage delicate bodies
pretending to know what to do, and singing.

www.ingramcontent.com/pod-product-compliance
Lightning Source LLC
Chambersburg PA
CBHW022123090426
42743CB00008B/983